VOL I

HELPMEET
Prayers for her
KING

Warfare Prayers to Cover Your Husband

YVETTE BENTON

Helpmeet Prayers for Her King: Warfare Prayers to Cover Your Husband

Copyright © 2021 Yvette Benton

All rights reserved. No part of this book may be used or reproduced, stored in a retrieval system or transmitted in any way by any means, electronic, mechanical, photocopy, recording or otherwise without the prior permission of the authors.

Help for The Helpmeet, Inc.

Kennesaw, GA

Assisted by: Global Destiny Enterprises, LLC

Cover Design by Angela Mills Camper of Dezign Pro Printing & Graphics

King James Version (KJV)

Public Domain

Amplified Bible (AMP)

Copyright © 2015 by The Lockman Foundation, La Habra, CA 90631. All rights reserved.

New King James Version (NKJV)

Scripture taken from the New King James Version®. Copyright © 1982 by Thomas Nelson. Used by permission. All rights reserved.

First Printing, 2021

ISBN: 978-1-7346335-1-1

Table of Contents

Introduction

My King's Hope	1
My King's Identity	9
My King's Balance	17
My King's Voice	27
My King's Deliverance	37
My King's Health	45
My King's Wisdom	53
My King's Vision	61
My King's Destiny	69
My King's Spiritual Growth	75
My King's Heart	81
My King's Strength	89
About the Author	97
Contact	99

Introduction

Helpmeet Prayers for Her King is a war tool for Helpmeets worldwide to cover their husbands in prayer. Its objective is to help women who do not know how to pray for their Kings' success in their God-given assignments. Satan wants our husbands to fail. It is his honor to distract our Kings from their purpose. However, God has mandated wives to fully operate in their roles as Helpmeets to cover their husbands in prayer consistently. In doing so, they help abort satan's plans for their husbands.

This prayer book is designed to motivate and activate wives to pray strategically for their husbands, to be fully-armed and battle-ready to launch their Kings on the earth. Prayer is a strategy from heaven to align ourselves with the will of God. Helpmeets, the wisdom of God is your portion. Let the prayers in this book activate your prayer life for your King.

My King's Hope

My King's name is_____.

Key Scripture*: "May the God of hope fill you with all joy and peace in believing [through the experience of your faith] that by the power of the Holy Spirit you will abound in hope and overflow with confidence in His promises"* (Romans 15:13, AMP).

Declaration*:* I decree and declare that my King abounds in hope. He is filled with joy and peace because he hopes in the Lord.

Helpmeet Prayer

God, I am reporting for duty. I am prepared to hear Your instructions, to come into agreement with Your will, pray, and ask for forgiveness. Lord God, I am asking for blessings and favor. I am the vessel You use to create a hedge of protection around my King, family, and me, in the name of Jesus. Father, forgive me of my sins as far as the east is from the west.

I am thankful, Lord God, for that forgiveness. Create in me a clean heart, oh God, and renew a right spirit within me *(Psalm 51:10)*. Your Word declares the effectual, fervent prayer of the righteous avails much *(James 5:16)*. Lord, whatever is on Your mind, whatever Holy Spirit tells me, I will obey. Lord God, I praise You for doing a new thing in my marriage. Transform me, Lord, in the same areas I pray for my King. Let us both be in one accord to fulfill Your purpose on the earth.

Right now, because we are one, I put the whole armor of God on my King and myself. I put on our helmets of salvation, our breastplates of righteousness, and our loins are girded with truth. Our feet are shod with the preparation of the gospel of peace *(Ephesians 6:11)*. Our shield of faith is in one hand, and our sword of the Spirit, which is the Word of God, is in the other. We have our armor on. I am ready for battle. None of the arrows the enemy throws at me will prevail. I am covered under the blood of Jesus. The weapons may form, but they will not prosper *(Isaiah 54:17)*. No scheme, plot, or plan the enemy tries to use to stop me will get past my prayers because I am prepared, and God has my back. In the name of Jesus, I dispatch angels to cover and protect me as I cover my King. God, I thank You that I have the authority to dispatch angels on behalf of my Priest, Prophet, and King (PPK). I thank You for positioning me as a Helpmeet suitable to pray for my King's hope.

Prayer for My King

Father, thank You for nudging me to pray for my King's hope today. God, I am following Your instructions. Your Word declares that faith is the substance of things hoped for and the evidence of things not seen (*Hebrews 11:1*). If my King has no hope, he cannot have faith.

Today, in the name of Jesus, I am speaking hope over my Priest, Prophet, and King. The leader of my home is covered in hope. He breathes hope, in the matchless name of Jesus. I decree and declare I have hope as a Helpmeet to provide that very hope to my King. God, I am ready to be of service to my King and speak hope to his present and future. I speak the substance of hope in my King's life; my King will not lack hope. I declare that when my King has hope in the Lord, he can do all things through Christ, which gives him strength (*Philippians 4:13*).

I decree and declare that my King has a great future, one he hopes for in You, Lord. I declare Jeremiah 29:11 over my King's future, in the name of Jesus. Lord, I thank You that my King will not be shameful but hopeful. My King will not be connected to failure but hope.

I pull down and bind the assignment of shame now in the name of Jesus! My King will not be embarrassed, but he will be confident in what the Lord is speaking to him. My King's past will not determine his hope. The devil is a liar; my King will abound in hope.

I set ablaze the spirit of shame; my King is being healed now from traumatic experiences, in the name of Jesus. The assignment of shame has been eradicated. Father, thank You for forgiving my King of sins that were committed in his past. As You forgive him, allow him to forgive those who have hurt him.

Decree: My King will not have shame. My King will not be hindered by shame. My King will not be stopped or slowed down by any shame because he is forgiven.

My King is covered in the blood of Jesus. I expose satan and his tricks, which are intended to fool my husband and cause him shame. My King's hope will not be deferred; he is experiencing hope now! In the name of Jesus, I pour out hope on my King. He is full of it. My King's hope is in the Word of God. Holy Spirit releases his hope. Father, I speak a spirit of gladness into my King. I decree and declare he will have increased hope.

Father, I know my husband is a Priest, Prophet, and King. He is a great King, in the name of Jesus. I have hope that my King can carry out his calling and fulfill his purpose. The hardness of my King's heart is now turned into flesh (*Ezekiel 36:26*).

I come against the spirit of depression that tries to take my King's hope. Depression, your assignment to cause a lack of hope and purpose is destroyed. My King will hope and not fear because the Lord is on his side. My King is covered. Angels are encamped around him. I pray that my King will have a supernatural amount of hope that will cause him to have a heart full of hope.

I thank You, God, that when he receives more hope, he can trust in You. Lord, he will have a heart of forgiveness. The lack of forgiveness causes him to speak from a place of defeat, shame, embarrassment, and hindrances. But no longer. I cut it off! He will speak from the pureness of his heart and a place of hope. He has desires in the Lord.

Hallelujah! Hope is my King's portion.

Hope is making my King strong. Hope is my King's foundation. Hope is my King's great substance.

Thank You, Lord, that my King is equipped and ready to speak over his family. My King is free to prophesy the will of the Lord.

My King is lined up with the perfect timing of God. He is not missing or late for his destiny. He is not late for favor; he is not late in responding to God. He is obedient. God, thank You, for knowing where my King is supposed to be. He has hope in You, Lord.

That assignment of helplessness and hopelessness has been sent back to the pit of hell in the name of Jesus. My King will not be blinded by helplessness or hopelessness. He will have the hope and help he needs to believe, trust, know, and understand God, in Jesus' name. In the book of Genesis, God said that Kings need help. I am the help, his Helpmeet. He will feel like a man, a King.

God, I thank You for revelation, wisdom, insight, and knowledge of what the enemy tries to do. He is no match for a Helpmeet suitable who knows her authority.

Lord, I thank You that my King's hope has been fully restored. In the name of Jesus, Amen.

As a Helpmeet suitable, how can you help your husband remain hopeful?

My King's Identity

My King's name is_____.

Key Scripture: *"So God created man in His own image, in the image and likeness of God He created him; male and female He created them" (Genesis 1:27, AMP).*

Declaration: I decree that my King's identity is being restored to the image of God. My King was created in the image and likeness of God. His identity is in Christ Jesus.

Helpmeet Prayer

God, I am reporting for duty. I am prepared to hear Your instructions, to come into agreement with Your will, pray, and ask for forgiveness. Lord God, I am asking for blessings and favor. I am Your vessel that is creating a hedge of protection around my King, family, and me, in the name of Jesus. Father, forgive me of my sins as far as the east is from the west.

I am thankful, Lord God, for that forgiveness. Create in me a clean heart and renew a right spirit within me (*Psalm 51:10*). Your Word declares the effectual fervent prayer of the righteous avails much *(James 5:16)*. Lord, whatever is on Your mind, whatever Holy Spirit tells me I will obey. Lord God, I praise You for doing a new thing in my marriage. Transform me, Lord, in the same areas I pray for my King. Let us both be in one accord to fulfill Your purpose on the earth.

Right now, because we are one, I put the whole armor of God on my King and myself. I put on our helmet of salvation, our breastplate of righteousness, and our loins are girded with truth. Moreover, our feet are shod with the preparation of the gospel of peace (*Ephesians 6:11*). Our shield of faith is in one hand, and our sword of the Spirit, which is the Word of God, is in the other hand. We have our armor on, and I am ready for battle. No arrow the enemy tries to throw at me will prevail. I am covered under the blood of Jesus. The weapons may form, but they will not prosper *(Isaiah 54:17)*. No scheme, plot, or plan the enemy tries to use to stop me will get past my prayers because I am prepared, and God has my back. In the name of Jesus, I dispatch angels to cover and protect me as I cover my King. God, I thank You that I have the authority to dispatch angels on behalf of my Priest, Prophet, and King (PPK). God, I thank You for positioning me as a Helpmeet suitable to pray for my King's identity.

Prayer for My King

In the name of Jesus, I am coming for the enemy who has tried to steal my King's identity. I am not having it. Father, cover him with Your blood.

Father, I know my King may have lost his identity in the world due to sin or trauma. I snatch back my King's true identity, in the name of Jesus. I dispatch angels on behalf of my King. I decree and declare he knows who he is. Nothing will stop my Priest, Prophet, and King from operating in his role and who he is. Nothing will stop my King from being the true individual, the true man of God, and the true kingdom man You have called him to be. God, I thank You that my King (insert husband's name) operates as a priest. I thank You that my King can and will speak over his family. My King's words have power. I am pulling back the identity satan tried to steal. My King's voice will not be silent or shamed. I decree and declare the identity of my King is restored. The identity my King was formed with in his mother's womb is restored. I thank You, Lord God, that You have called my husband a King. He was created a King. He was created a priest over his family.

Thank You, Lord, that my King knows how to intercede for his family. He knows how to come to You, Father, to receive revelation, information, and instructions. My King comes boldly to the throne of grace *(Hebrews 4:16),* knowing his role and identity. He is aware and sober-minded concerning the things of God. I decree and declare we are a kingdom family. I declare that my husband is a kingdom husband. He is a kingdom man. My King will be the man of God he was called to be. My husband will operate as a priest; he will function as a prophet. My King will open his mouth wide, and the Lord will fill it *(Psalm 81:10).* I bind every assignment of the enemy that causes my Priest, Prophet, and King to forget the Word of God. My King will remember his instructions from God and carry them out with boldness. I speak boldness to my King to walk in his identity. I speak strength over him and pronounce he is the prophetic voice in his home. I decree that nothing will hinder him from speaking to my Priest, Prophet, and King's identity. God, I thank You that my King understands who he is in You. I crush every assignment of the enemy that tries to stop him from being in the position and role You set before him. My King is a worshipper. He is a man of valor. He will not be hindered by anything satan puts in front of him.

My King is not an addict. He will not be addicted to anything but God. My King is recovering from all addictions, in the name of Jesus. My King is no longer bound. He is walking in his identity. My King will not be hindered by alcohol or drugs. My King is everything God created him to be. His identity is intact. My King will not be in shackles or behind bars in the spirit or naturally that will cause him to be bound. I release him now in the name of Jesus! My King is not gay; he is not a homosexual. I bind the spirit of perversion. He is not adulterous. He is not a fornicator. These sins are not his identity. He will follow the will of God. I pray my King will have a repentant heart. He is pure and holy, in the name of Jesus. My King understands the truth and is walking in it. The truth will set him free (*John 8:32*). My King's identity will represent Jesus Christ. My King will know his sonship in Christ and come forth, in the name of Jesus.

My King will be identified as a kingdom citizen, a kingdom man, a kingdom father, and a kingdom husband. I declare his identity will come forth. Rise up, King, and declare the glory of the Lord. My King will be identified as an intercessor. My King will stand in the gap for his family. My King is a watchman on the wall. I speak to his mind so he understands his identity. I decree he will walk in his identity with power. I release the promises of God over his identity. Because my King knows his identity, he will walk in favor; unexpected doors will open.

I break every stronghold that tries to hold my husband back from his true identity. My King has the capacity to walk in healing and deliverance to move in his ordained purpose. Father, give my King knowledge, wisdom, discernment, and insight into their identity. I crush word curses that come against his identity. I reverse the curse and eradicate it in the spirit realm.

No weapon will be formed against my King's identity. My King is an overcomer, in the name of Jesus. Past trauma will not identify him. God adopted my King; he is not an orphan. My husband will understand his position in the kingdom of God. My King is a son of God. He is accepted and loved. I decree and declare that my King is fearfully and wonderfully made *(Psalm 139:14)*. My King will have a godly perspective and personality. My King will know who he is in the spirit and walk in his identity. I declare he will walk in his true calling, under an open heaven, and in his divine identity.

My King will press toward the mark of the high calling (*Philippians 3:14*). Every mountain is being removed from my King's identity. Father, not only will my husband know who he is created to be, I will know who he is also. Teach and reveal to me the identity of my King. Generational curses, strange fire, and hindering spirits are not his identity in the name of Jesus. As a Helpmeet suitable, I will not speak anything opposite of my King's identity. I will speak righteous words over him. I create a hedge of protection around him and his identity. God, deliver me if I am a hindrance to my husband. God, forgive me. There will be no backlash or retaliation to this prayer and revelation. I understand my King's identity, and I speak forth fruit, in Jesus' name. I declare that my King is in position. Amen.

God, I thank You for revelation, wisdom, insight, and knowledge of what the enemy is trying to do. The enemy is no match for a Helpmeet suitable who knows her authority.

As a Helpmeet suitable, how can you help your husband walk in his true identity?

My King's Balance

My King's name is_____.

Key Scripture: *"Being a double-minded man, unstable and restless in all his ways [in everything he thinks, feels, or decides"* (James 1:8, AMP).

Declaration: The life of my King is one of discipline. He will be naturally and spiritually balanced to fulfill the will of God. My King is stable in all his ways.

Helpmeet Prayer

God, I am reporting for duty. I am prepared to hear Your instructions, to come into agreement with Your will, pray, and ask for forgiveness. Lord God, I am asking for blessings and favor. I am Your vessel that is creating a hedge of protection around my King, family, and me, in the name of Jesus. Father, forgive me of my sins as far as the east is from the west.

I am thankful, Lord God, for Your forgiveness. Create in me

a clean heart and renew a right spirit within me (*Psalm 51:10*). Your Word declares the effectual, fervent prayer of the righteous avails much (*James 5:16*). Lord, whatever is on Your mind, whatever Holy Spirit tells me I will obey. Lord God, I praise You for doing a new thing in my marriage. Transform me, Lord, in the same areas I pray for my King. Let us both be in one accord to fulfill Your purpose on the earth.

Right now, because we are one, I put the whole armor of God on my King and myself. I put on our helmet of salvation, our breastplate of righteousness, and our loins are girded with truth. Our feet are shod with the preparation of the gospel of peace (*Ephesians 6:11*). Our shield of faith is in one hand, and our sword of the Spirit, which is the Word of God, is in the other hand. We have our armor on, and I am ready for battle. No arrow the enemy tries to throw at me will prevail. I am covered under the blood of Jesus. The weapons may form, but they will not prosper (*Isaiah 54:17*). No scheme, plot, or plan the enemy tries to use to stop me will get past my prayers because I am prepared. God has my back. In the name of Jesus, I dispatch angels to cover and protect me as I cover my King. God, I thank You that I have the authority to dispatch angels on behalf of my Priest, Prophet, and King (PPK). I thank You for positioning me as a Helpmeet suitable to pray for my King's balance.

Prayer for My King

Father, I come to You, in the name of Jesus Christ, standing in the gap for my King. I cover every area of his life with the blood. God, I break the spirit of imbalance from his life. Thank You, Lord, for bringing my husband into a mature state in You. I decree and declare that he is in a place of discipline and balance to receive instruction from God and handle the assignment.

No weapon formed against my King shall prosper, in the name of Jesus.

No generational curse will come after my King that the blood of Jesus cannot cover and the power of Holy Spirit cannot take away. I thank You, Lord, that You are raising me up as a Deborah in this hour. You are raising me up as a Helpmeet suitable.

In the name of Jesus, I am using my power and authority to bruise the head of satan. I decree and declare balance over my King. I decree and declare my King's mind is sound. I refuse as a Helpmeet suitable to allow my King's mind to race. I shut down the racing mind, as well as the attacks against the mind and thoughts of my King, in the name of Jesus. The mind of my King will be still and know You are God. I declare Psalm 46:10 (KJV) over my King: *"Be still and know that I am God: I will be exalted among the heathen. I will be exalted in the earth."*

I thank You, Lord, that my King understands true balance. I declare he will know how to be still. I declare that he will understand how to move in faith. My King will hear Your still, small voice. The Spirit of God will lead my King. He will be righteous and align with the will of God. I speak that my Priest, Prophet, and King has a balanced mind, and his thoughts are balanced.

My King's mind is moving from evil to good, in the name of

Jesus. I break any assignment that tries to come against the mind of my King. Any assignment that tries to knock him off balance is destroyed. I come after what causes my King's mind to be in unrest and anxiety. I come against the spirit of anxiety, PTSD, and post-traumatic stress disorder, in the name of Jesus. I cover the thoughts of my King. Father, in the name of Jesus, I protect the mind of my King and cover his thoughts in prayer. I declare my King will have a balanced mind when he is making decisions.

I decree and declare the mind of my King is connected to Holy Spirit to receive the revelation of God. I pray he will be stable in private and in public. My King will be stable in his thinking, sound in his mind, and steady in his thought process. I pray that my King will be stable in the things that are new to him. I thank You, Lord, that old things are passing away; behold, all things are new *(2 Corinthians 5:17)*. I pray that my King has the balance to understand not to hold on to things from his past but to press toward the mark for the prize of the high calling of God in Christ Jesus *(Philippians 3:14)*.

Father, I thank You that my King will not give in to the spirit of fear. I strike down fear, in the name of Jesus. I use the sword of the Spirit and sever every soul tie that causes him to fear, in the name of Jesus. My King will not go to what is familiar. He will go to what is right and not what he is used to. I sever every soul tie that is pulling my King back to poor decisions and flawed thinking. I speak balance to my King; he will receive new information with a balanced mind. Through balance, my King will hear instructions and walk them out properly. I decree and declare that the way for my King is clear. Lord, I come against every distraction and hindrance that tries to stop my King's balance. I bruise the head of satan with my heel.

As a Helpmeet suitable, I am locking arms with Holy Spirit, standing in unity and oneness. Father, in the name of Jesus, I align myself in the spirit. Father, show me my King in the spirit. Teach me how to pray for a balanced life for my King. Open his eyes that he may see the areas in need of balance. Old thoughts are canceled. There is a no return policy. Every generational curse is canceled; there is a no return policy. There is a no return policy on fear and anxiety. I return every attack with a boomerang back to the pit of hell.

My King will understand the Word of God; he will not perish for lack of knowledge *(Hosea 4:6)*. He will have knowledge of what happens in the spirit realm. Demons will not be able to return, in the name of Jesus. The eviction notice has been given, and there will be no return of evil on the King's mindset. I pray my King will walk and speak in obedience because obedience is better than sacrifice *(1 Samuel 15:22)*. My King is strong in the Lord. He has revelation and insight. My King is mature in the spirit. He has put away childish ways. *"When I was a child, I spake as a child, I understood as a child, I thought as a child: but when I became a man, I put away childish things" (1 Corinthians 13:11, KJV)*.

Everything the devil tried to take from my King, I am taking it back by force. Everything the devil tried to steal from us, our family, I take it back! In the name of Jesus, I decree and declare balance over my King's mind. I speak balance over his physical body. My King's heart is lining up with the will of the Father. Everything concerning my King is in perfect harmony. His bloodstream is lined up. His lymphatic system is lined up. His organs are balanced. His heart and immune system are balanced, in the name of Jesus. My King will balance everything concerning his body. I decree and declare that balance is his portion. Father, You said in Your Word if we decree a thing, it shall be established *(Job 22:28)*. I declare mental and spiritual balance. His energy levels are balanced, in the name of Jesus.

God, I thank You that my King's health is perfect; his mind is perfect. He has complete balance in all areas of his life. He will be balanced in how he studies the Word of God. My King will balance his time with his children. He is balancing and understanding how to work and play. My King will have balance in his schedule for his Helpmeet. He studies new things and practices discipline to maintain his balance. My King will have the ability to balance the wisdom that is given to him. He will have self-control and be balanced in his mind.

I declare a new balance is coming to my King. I declare supernatural balance over my King.

I tear down and cancel the assignment that causes imbalance.

My King is balanced in the Lord. I declare he is balanced in his finances. He is balanced in wealth. Imbalance has been in his life long enough; the spirit of imbalance is being exposed and defeated, in the name of Jesus. God, thank You for Your wisdom in catching the imbalance thief. Spirit of imbalance, you will no longer steal the balance of my King. I curse imbalance, in the name of Jesus. I destroy every demonic assignment of imbalance and decree that my King is in total alignment with You, Father. I decree and declare perfect alignment over my King. I speak perfect alignment of peace, wealth, wisdom, and knowledge. My King is perfectly aligned with the will of God, the ways of God and the Word of God. My King is in perfect alignment with his communication with God and his Helpmeet. I plead the blood of Jesus over my King's balance. I plead the blood of Jesus over his vision. I plead the blood of Jesus over his thoughts and mind. I decree and declare that my King will be bold; he has spiritual discernment and understanding. My King is spiritually sharp. He has the lion and lamb anointing.

Lord, I decree and declare my King is balanced and as a Helpmeet suitable, I will be balanced in every area of my life. I will not be ignorant of satan's devices. I will be wise as a serpent and harmless as a dove *(Matthew 10:16)*.

Thank You, Lord, that the spirit of imbalance has been uprooted and never to be seen again. I decree and declare that my King and I will be balanced in our prayer lives—the prayers of the righteous availeth much *(James 5:16)*. Father, heal me in every area that I have been hurt so I may walk in balance. I speak to angels to surround my King, "Angels, go forth to cover, protect, lead, and guide him." I send angels to cover my King while he keeps the balance he needs for the decisions God has trusted him with. My King is now walking in a new balance for his life.

In the mighty name of Jesus. Amen.

As a Helpmeet suitable, how can you help your husband balance work, home, and his time with God?

MY KING'S VOICE

My King's name is_____.

Key Scripture: *"Then the LORD stretched out His hand and touched my mouth, and the LORD said to me, "Behold (hear Me), I have put My words in your mouth" (Jeremiah 1:9, AMP).*

Deliverance: The voice of my King is spiritually activated. My King will speak the Word of the Lord.

Helpmeet Prayer

God, I am reporting for duty. I am ready and prepared to hear Your instructions, to come into agreement with Your will, pray, and ask for forgiveness. Lord God, I am asking for blessings and favor. I am Your vessel that is creating a hedge of protection around my King, family, and me, in the name of Jesus. Father, forgive me of my sins as far as the east is from the west.

I am thankful, Lord God, for that forgiveness. Create in me

a clean heart and renew a right spirit within me (*Psalm 51:10*). Your Word declares the effectual, fervent prayer of the righteous avails much *(James 5:16)*. Lord, whatever is on Your mind, whatever Holy Spirit tells me I will obey. Lord God, I praise You for doing a new thing in my marriage. Transform me, Lord, in the same areas I pray for my King. Let us both be in one accord to fulfill Your purpose on the earth.

Right now, because we are one, I put the whole armor of God on my King and myself. I put on our helmet of salvation, our breastplate of righteousness, and our loins are girded with truth. Our feet are shod with the preparation of the gospel of peace (*Ephesians 6:11*). Our shield of faith is in one hand, and our sword of the Spirit, which is the Word of God, is in the other hand. We have our armor on, and I am prepared for battle. No arrow the enemy tries to throw at me will prevail. I am covered under the blood of Jesus. The weapons may form, but they will not prosper *(Isaiah 54:17)*. No scheme, plot, or plan the enemy tries to use to stop me will get past my prayers because I am prepared, and God has my back. In the name of Jesus, I dispatch angels to cover and protect me as I cover my King. God, I thank You that I have the authority to dispatch angels on behalf of my Priest, Prophet, and King (PPK). Father, You told me to declare this is the year of the mouth. My King's voice is under attack, and I am praying against the assignment sent to destroy it. Give me strength, in Your name. God, I thank You for positioning me as a Helpmeet suitable to pray for my King's voice.

Prayer for My King

Father, in the name of Jesus, I dispatch angels on behalf of my King. Father, I pray for the voice of my King. As his Helpmeet, I have the authority and power to lift up my King's voice. This is the decade of the mouth. This is the decade where I can have what I say and so can my King. Satan, you will not muzzle the Helpmeets; you will not muzzle our words. You will not muzzle our prayers. You will not muzzle the things God has told us to say. Father, when we open our mouths to prayer for our Kings, fill them. I speak to the voice of my King and say that his voice will be heard in the earth realm. I thank You, Father, that my King will cry aloud and spare not *(Isaiah 58:1)*. My King will open his mouth wide, and the Lord will fill it *(Psalm 81:10)*. The mouth of my King will not be filled with foolishness but with the glory of the Lord.

I shut down every assignment of the enemy. I close the gap, in the name of Jesus. My King will not speak the enemy's words but will speak the Word of God, in Jesus' name. I nullify spoken curses against my King's mouth. I speak now, in the name of Jesus that my King experiences an upgrade in his voice. My King has revelation, wisdom, knowledge, and insight. He is speaking to the Lord in boldness and confidence. His voice will be heard all over the world, and when it is, he will be heard speaking the Word of the Lord. My King will be heard declaring the revelation of God. My King will speak the truth, and when he does, he will continuously walk-in freedom. I speak truth out of the mouth of my King. Even if I hear a lie, I will not be disrespectful or dishonorable. I will honor my King. I will pray about the lie and speak the truth. I will not call my King a liar, but I will continue to declare the truth out of the mouth of my King.

I speak that my King's heart is right because out of the

abundance of the heart, the mouth speaks *(Luke 6:45)*. So, I speak to the heart of my King, in the name of Jesus. Father, posture the heart of my King, so he speaks godliness. Father, I pray that my King's heart is fixed toward You so his words are godly and his heart says exactly what You have laid on it, in the name of Jesus. Father, I pray that when my King speaks the Word of God, his words penetrate darkness and demonic assignments, in the name of Jesus. I speak an upgrade to my King's voice, now. I speak an upgrade to his words. I speak spiritual strength to his voice, in the name of Jesus. My King is opening his mouth, decreeing, and declaring the will of God, and it shall be established *(Job 22:28)*. My King is decreeing and declaring over his family.

Father, use my King's voice to create and declare his purpose and destiny. Father, I thank You that my King's voice is bold and courageous. He is not afraid of what You have given him to speak. He is not afraid of what You have revealed to him in dreams and visions. Father, I set the atmosphere in my home that is conducive for my King to speak, in the name of Jesus. I send a Holy Ghost bomb to every circumstance that causes my King to feel as if he cannot speak openly. I declare you can speak Priest, Prophet, and King. You can speak boldly. You can speak courageously. You can speak loudly. You can speak what God has said, in the name of Jesus.

My King has an atmosphere at home where he feels safe to speak. He is covered. Lord, forgive me if I have not created this conducive atmosphere for my husband; help me to get it right. This is the decade of the mouth. Therefore, I declare that my King will speak because he is the head. And I know certain things will not be established until my King opens his mouth. His voice is loud. His voice is honorable. His Voice speaks the Word of God. I thank You, Father, that when my King hears Your voice, a stranger's voice he will not follow *(John 10:5)*. My husband will hear Your voice and speak what He has heard, in the name of Jesus.

My King has an empowering voice and word to release into the atmosphere. He covers our family, destiny, and me in prayer. My King is praying without ceasing *(1 Thessalonians 5:17)*; he sings songs of worship and opens his mouth wide. Lord, I thank You that my King has been ungraded in his praise and worship. He is singing songs of praise, songs of worship, and prophetic songs. The prophetic voice of my husband is coming forth. The King in my husband is arising, and he will be a respected prophetic voice in the land. His voice will be heard and honored. Open your mouth, my King, and speak what the Lord is saying.

I crush the laryngitis spirit that tries to silence my King's voice, in the name of Jesus; you have not lost your voice. Satan is afraid of your voice, but you will not back down. Keep your mouth wide open.

I shut down COVID-19 and bind its purpose of trying to stop the breath of the Kings. My King will not lose his voice. The voice of my King will lead, be bold, and be heard. My King (Insert husband's name here) will speak deliverance over the nations, and his voice is established on the earth. I take the sword of the Spirit and cut every soul tie that is causing hindrances to the tongue. My King will pray in tongues and speak in new tongues. My King will not be ignorant of satan's devices.

I pull down the stronghold of shame over my King's life; he will not be silent. Today, my King is free. Today, he speaks his way out of bondage.

I thank You, Lord God, that cycles have been broken because my King is speaking. Generational curses are broken because my King is speaking. My King knows his worth; he knows who he is. There is no condemnation for past mistakes. My King is covered—no shame! In the name of Jesus, I speak into the destiny of my King and say go forth. My King's heart is right before God. Every demonic cord trying to wrap itself around the neck of my King is broken.

Lord, forgive me if I have done anything to shut down the voice of my King. He will not suffocate in his own home. He will speak, "Thus, says the Lord." My King's voice is anointed. I pull down false voices. As Helpmeet to my King, I take the sword of Spirit with precision and cut the enemy's assignment. I will cut the enemy's voice but not the voice of my King. I will not hinder my King with my voice. My voice is anointed. My voice is sweet. My voice will be of aid to my King.

In the name of Jesus, I set ablaze childhood trauma that has tried to silence my King's voice. The hand that has been over the Priest, Prophet, and King's mouth is being destroyed right now. Every hand that has tried to silence his voice through childhood trauma is removed. I remove the hand of trauma and abuse. I declare that this generational curse will not return. I speak a Helpmeet hedge around my King, a hedge of protection.

I cover my household with the blood of Jesus. The blood of Jesus covers my Priest, Prophet, and King. I cast down arguments and every high thing that exalts itself against the knowledge of God. I bring into captivity every thought to the obedience of Christ *(2 Corinthians 10:5)*. I will embrace my King's voice at home. I come against backlash and retaliation. Nothing is missing. Nothing is lacking in my King. My King will have what he says. My King's voice stops demonic assignments against the voice of other men on the earth.

The assignment of my King's voice is being fulfilled. The voice of my King has been set free. There is a new sound coming out of his voice. In the name of Jesus, Amen!

As a Helpmeet suitable, how can you help in making sure your husband's voice is heard at home and in the kingdom of God?

My King's Deliverance

My King's name is _____.

Key Scripture: *"For He has rescued us and has drawn us to Himself from the dominion of darkness, and has transferred us to the kingdom of His beloved Son" (Colossians 1:13, AMP).*

Deliverance: My King is delivered from darkness and transferred into the kingdom of God.

Helpmeet Prayer

God, I am reporting for duty. I am ready to hear Your instructions, come into agreement with Your will, pray, and ask for forgiveness. Lord God, I am asking for blessings and favor. I am Your vessel that is creating a hedge of protection around my King, family, and me, in the name of Jesus. Father, forgive me of my sins as far as the east is from the west.

I am thankful, Lord God, for that forgiveness. Create in me a clean heart and renew a right spirit within me (*Psalm 51:10*). Your Word declares the effectual, fervent prayer of the righteous avails much *(James 5:16)*. Lord, whatever is on Your mind, whatever Holy Spirit tells me I will obey. Lord God, I praise You for doing a new thing in my marriage. Transform me, Lord, in the same areas I pray for my King. Let us both be in one accord to fulfill Your purpose on the earth.

Right now, because we are one, I put the whole armor of God on my King and myself. I put on our helmet of salvation, our breastplate of righteousness and our loins are girded about with truth. Our feet are shod with the preparation of the gospel of peace (*Ephesians 6:11*). Our shield of faith is in one hand, and our sword of the Spirit, which is the Word of God, is in the other hand. We have our armor on, and I am prepared for battle. No arrow the enemy tries to throw at me will prevail. I am covered under the blood of Jesus. The weapons may form, but they will not prosper *(Isaiah 54:17)*. No scheme, plot, or plan the enemy tries to use to stop me will get past my prayers because I am prepared, and God has my back. In the name of Jesus, I dispatch angels to cover and protect me as I cover my King. God, I thank You that I have the authority to dispatch angels on behalf of my Priest, Prophet, and King (PPK). I stand firm in praying for my King's deliverance with honor and respect. God, I thank You for positioning me as a Helpmeet suitable to pray for my King's deliverance.

Prayer for My King

Oh, God, my Deliverer. I come to You on behalf of my King.

I pray that anything hindering my prayers from being heard or answered will be removed from my life. I refuse to pray amiss. So, God, get my heart right. I put myself in a position to have my heart right. My heart is wholly given to You, in Jesus' name. I trust You, Lord, with my whole heart. I lean not to my own understanding but acknowledge You in all my ways (*Proverbs 3:5-6*). Father, I come to You today to cover my King's deliverance. Teach me how to honor my King and pray for deliverance and continued deliverance. God, first and foremost, You are the King of kings and You told me to respect and honor my husband. I appreciate and honor my King before You. As I spend more time with You, Father, teach me how to honor my King and show him respect. Father, thank You for forgiving me for treating my King as anything less than what You have called him to be. Father, I am a clean vessel ready to be used by You. I come to You pure, holy, and righteous. Your Word declares that the effectual fervent prayers of the righteous availeth much (*James 5:16*).

Lord God, I praise You for my King's deliverance. I am praying for my King to be delivered and set free. I decree and declare that he is a set-free vessel. I thank You, Lord, that the things of the past do not hinder my King. I speak deliverance, in the name of Jesus. My King will be set free and not hindered by his thoughts, trauma, or generational curses. God, I thank You for being like a surgeon in the spirit, and I am Your Helpmeet assistant. I will assist in making sure everything within my King is clean and protected. I decree and declare there will be no residue or stone unturned. I lock arms with Holy Spirit and come in agreement with the deliverance of the Lord over my King's life. I walk in the authority You have given me to trample on serpents and scorpions and over all the power of the enemy. Nothing shall by any means hurt me (*Luke 10:19*).

God, thank You for giving us the physical and mental strength, the ability to have all power over the enemy. I pull down strongholds that will try to hinder the deliverance of my King. I declare that my husband will be delivered from fear today. For God has not given us a spirit of fear but of power and of love and of a sound mind (*2 Timothy 1:7, NJKV*). There is no fear of failure. I declare that fear is replaced with faith. I decree that my husband is a successful King. In every area of my King's life, he will be successful. My King is successful in his mindset; he will see the transformation in his mind. My King is a mighty warrior in the kingdom of God.

I am decreeing the successful deliverance from addictions: drugs, alcohol, smoking, perversion, pride, gangs, arrested development, and idolatry. My King will press toward the mark for the prize of the high calling of God in Christ Jesus. He is pressing toward his deliverance, and he will not stop until he is completely delivered (*Philippians 3:14*). I will completely support my King in his deliverance. I declare victory over every assignment of the enemy that has been planted to destroy the deliverance of my King.

I close the mouth of the enemy and cancel any noise and every demonic distraction. May my prayers as a Helpmeet be louder than any distraction of the enemy. I cancel any inappropriate behavior that led my King to need deliverance. I declare that my King will fully submit to God and resist the devil (*James 4:7*). The bloodline of my King is being delivered now, in the name of Jesus. The full armor of God protects my King. I loose angels to help and aid in my King's deliverance. God, I thank You for being the Lord of the breakthrough. There will be no relapse; my King will not backslide. My King will move forward in his deliverance.

Father, thank You for giving me the heart to believe in my King. Nothing is impossible with Him. Father, help me to encourage my King through the process of his deliverance. Thank You for grace and mercy. I pray that my body language, facial expressions, and words will not hinder my King's process. I decree and declare that my King is set free. Although my natural eyes might see differently. I believe in the deliverance of my King.

Lord, open my King's eyes. Rip off the confusion and allow the scales to be removed so he can receive his full deliverance. My King will see the full promises of God for his life. He will see the enemy afar off and be alert to any of his tricks. I decree and declare that my King is established in God. He will believe in his deliverance. I bind the cycle of sin; it is broken! In the name of Jesus, I declare that no weapon formed against my King will prosper, and every tongue that rises against him in judgment, You, God, shall condemn *(Isaiah 54:17)*. I set a trap for the enemy with my prayers, the anointing, and the blood of Jesus. I decree and declare that my King and I are warriors in the spirit realm. The devil is defeated. I speak the fire of God on generational curses.

I pray that every addiction will be replaced with holy living and a righteous mindset. My King will walk in holiness, peace, and righteousness. Lord, Your Word declares in *Psalm 34:17* that the righteous cry out, and You hear and deliver them out of all their troubles. My King is delivered. My King is a friend of God. Father, walk my husband through his deliverance. Let him see Your hand in his transformation. My King is a chosen vessel. He is a kingdom man; his behavior models the kingdom of God. My King is walking in victory. I believe, Lord, that Your plan for my King is perfect. I decree and declare that my King walks in *Jeremiah 29:11* daily. *"'For I know the plans I have for you,' declares the LORD, 'plans to prosper you and not to harm you, plans to give you hope and a future.'"* He will walk in blessings and favor the rest of his life.

I declare recompense; it is not enough just for my King to be delivered. I declare full payback. Everything that was stolen is being returned to our household. May we be paid back a thousand-fold. I am coming after the thief that steals, kills, and destroys, in the name of Jesus. My marriage and legacy are fully restored, in the name of Jesus. I decree and declare that You, Lord, are my King's hiding place. You preserve him from trouble and surround him with songs of deliverance *(Psalm 32:7).*

I decree and declare, in the name of Jesus, that deliverance is my King's portion. Amen.

As a Helpmeet suitable, how can you help your husband start and maintain his deliverance?

MY KING'S HEALTH

My King's name is_____.

Key Scripture: *"For I will restore health to you, And I will heal your wounds,' says the Lord, Because they have called you an outcast, saying: "This is Zion; no one seeks her and no one cares for her" (Jeremiah 30:17, AMP).*

Declaration: I decree and declare that my King's health is restored. My King will live and not die.

Helpmeet Prayer

God, I am reporting for duty. I am prepared to hear Your instructions, to come into agreement with Your will, pray, and ask for forgiveness. Lord God, I am asking for blessings and favor. I am Your vessel that is creating a hedge of protection around my King, family, and me, in the name of Jesus. Father, forgive me of my sins as far as the east is from the west.

I am thankful, Lord God, for that forgiveness. Create in me

a clean heart and renew a right spirit within me (*Psalm 51:10*). Your Word declares the effectual, fervent prayer of the righteous avails much *(James 5:16)*. Lord, whatever is on Your mind, whatever Holy Spirit tells me I will obey. Lord God, I praise You for doing a new thing in my marriage. Transform me, Lord, in the same areas I pray for my King. Let us both be in one accord to fulfill Your purpose on the earth.

Right now, because we are one, I put the whole armor of God on my King, and myself. I put on our helmet of salvation, our breastplate of righteousness, and our loins are girded with truth. Our feet are shod with the preparation of the gospel of peace (*Ephesians 6:11*). Our shield of faith is in one hand, and our sword of the Spirit, which is the Word of God, is in the other hand. We have our armor on, and I am ready for battle. No arrow the enemy tries to throw at me will prevail. I am covered under the blood of Jesus. The weapons may form, but they will not prosper *(Isaiah 54:17)*. No scheme, plot, or plan the enemy tries to use to stop me will get past my prayers because I am prepared, and God has my back. In the name of Jesus, I dispatch angels to cover and protect me as I cover my King. God, I thank You that I have the authority to dispatch angels on behalf of my Priest, Prophet, and King (PPK). God, I thank You for positioning me as a Helpmeet suitable to pray for my King's health.

Prayer for My King

Father, in the name of Jesus, I lift the health of my King to You, Jehovah Rapha, the God who heals. I am calling on You today to be ever so present in the area of my King's health. I decree and declare Psalm 91 over my King and family. As I am dwelling in the secret place, shield us from anything harmful to our health, in the name of Jesus. Lord, cover my King in Your armor. Protect him from backlash and retaliation. Lord, thank You for providing us both with the weaponry to fight and protect our family *(Ephesians 6:10-20)*.

Lord, I am Your intercessor; whatever You speak to me about my King, I will seek You in prayer concerning it. Father, I thank You that the health of my King is on Your heart and mind. I decree and declare the Word of God over the health of my King, in Jesus' name. I pray that my King's body will line up correctly with how God designed it. Bloodstream, line up! In the name of Jesus, I speak to the heart of my King and say, "Pump correctly." I bind every assignment of heart issues or heart disease, in Jesus' name. I say that my King's heart is pure. Not only is his heart pure spiritually, but it is also cleansed in the natural. Father, I thank You that my King's heart is working properly in the physical realm. I cancel the enemy's assignment causing any disease to come upon the body of my King. I bind COVID-19, in the name of Jesus. There will be no hindrances to my King's body, no impediment to his breathing. I speak that my King's lungs are clear. I bind the assignment of poor breathing, in Jesus' name. My King can breathe; he is breathing. I bind the assignment and curse on the earth that says that our Kings cannot breathe. No weapon formed against my King will prosper *(Isaiah 54:17)*.

Father, Your Word says that death and life are in the power of the tongue *(Proverbs 18:21)*. I bind any assignment of death that is trying to connect itself to my King. My King will live and not die. I bind the spirit of premature death. My

King will do exactly what God has called him forth to do on the earth. Premature death, Your assignment has been canceled off my King's bloodline, in the name of Jesus. No weapon formed against my King will prosper. I decree and declare that generational diseases no longer hinder my King. They will no longer hinder the family because my King is anointed. Sickness and disease will no longer hinder my King or family because of prayer.

Father, with the shield of faith and the sword of the Spirit, I pull down and cancel the assignment of high blood pressure. My King will not have heart issues. He is healthy; he will live a long and prosperous life. My King's organs are fully functioning and operating to the utmost level of excellence. Father, I speak spiritual dialysis to cleanse the body of my King, in Jesus' name. Lord, cleanse my King with the blood of Jesus. Father, cover the spiritual and physical health of my King. Let him be healthy in both areas, Lord, with no hindrances.

I crush premature death. I go after it; there will be no premature death because of generational curses. There will be no premature death because of accidents or incidents. There will be no premature death because of work problems, in Jesus' name. I decree and declare that my husband's appetite is changing; he will have excellent eating habits. My King will desire to change his diet. He will desire to eat fruits and veggies. Lord, I thank You that my King will have a renewed mindset concerning eating healthy and being fit for this kingdom assignment. My King will desire a healthy routine for exercise and enjoy it. I decree and declare that my King is in perfect emotional health.

Father, good sleep patterns are considered healthy. I pray that my King will not be hindered by the assignment of insomnia and sleep apnea. Lord, Your Word declares that You give Your beloved rest *(Psalm 127:2)*. I speak over my King sweet sleep. I speak spiritual alignment over my King and that he is walking in perfect health. My King will no longer deal with the spirit of anxiety and worry that causes mental breakdowns and seizures. Depression has no place in the life of my King. The assignment of headaches to cause distractions is destroyed. My King will balance stress appropriately without it affecting him mentally, physically, and emotionally. I speak to my King's equilibrium and say, "Line up, now!" There will be no traces of dizziness. My King is free of all mental disorders. He will live and think properly. In the name of Jesus, my King will understand what is best for him and his family.

My King will not be weary in well-doing. He will be balanced and full of energy. He will be fully aware of his body's proper vitamins; he will have no vitamin deficiencies. His testosterone levels are appropriate. All his vitamin levels are equal. My King's hormone levels are balanced. I bind the usage of illegal drugs and addictions. I cancel generational cycles that cause my King to be addicted to salt and sugar. My King's spirit and body will be rejuvenated. No disease will come near the dwelling of my King.

The immune system of my King is perfectly aligned with the will of God. I bind the assignment of cancer. I command it to leave and never return. The cardiovascular and digestive systems of my King are covered under the blood. Any sickness that is in the body of my King has been served an eviction notice. It is time to go cancer, asthma, STDs, PTSD, bipolar, and COVID-19. The intimacy that was ordained for my husband and me is covered under the blood; there will be no issues with these organs. Father, restore everything in my husband's body that is not aligned with Your Word. God, I burn up everything outside of Your will with fire. My King is receiving new strength to his body now, in the name of Jesus. Restoration is my King's portion.

My King's mind is restored to health. The stripes of Jesus healed my King. Jehovah Rapha, the God who heals, thank You, for healing my King. He is set free and delivered. The testimony for my King is the doctor will say the test is negative. My King has overcome by the blood of the Lamb and the word of his testimony *(Revelation 12:11)*. His testimony is that he is healthy and healed by the precious blood of Jesus. Amen.

As a Helpmeet suitable, how can you help your husband practice remaining in good health?

My King's Wisdom

My King's name is_____.

Key Scripture: *"For the LORD gives [skillful and godly] wisdom; From His mouth come knowledge and understanding"* (Proverbs 2:6, AMP).

Declaration: I decree and declare that my King will receive wisdom from Lord. I declare that he will have the knowledge and understanding to use the wisdom downloaded from God.

Helpmeet Prayer

God, I am reporting for duty. I am prepared to hear Your instructions, to come into agreement with Your will, pray, and ask for forgiveness. Lord God, I am asking for blessings and favor. I am Your vessel that is creating a hedge of protection around my King, family, and me, in the name of Jesus. Father, forgive me of my sins as far as the east is from the west.

I am thankful, Lord God, for that forgiveness. Create in me a clean heart and renew a right spirit within me (*Psalm 51:10*). Your Word declares the effectual, fervent prayer of the righteous avails much *(James 5:16)*. Lord, whatever is on Your mind, whatever Holy Spirit tells me I will obey. Lord God, I praise You for doing a new thing in my marriage. Transform me, Lord, in the same areas I pray for my King. Let us both be in one accord to fulfill Your purpose on the earth.

Right now, because we are one, I put the whole armor of God on my King and myself. I put on our helmet of salvation, our breastplate of righteousness, and our loins are girded about with truth. Our feet are shod with the preparation of the gospel of peace (*Ephesians 6:11*). Our shield of faith is in one hand, and our sword of the Spirit, which is the Word of God, is in the other hand. We have our armor on, and I am ready for the battle. No arrow the enemy tries to throw at me will prevail. I am covered under the blood of Jesus. The weapons may form, but they will not prosper *(Isaiah 54:17)*. No scheme, plot, or plan the enemy tries to use to stop me will get past my prayers because I am prepared, and God has my back. In the name of Jesus, I dispatch angels to cover and protect me as I cover my King. God, I thank You that I have the authority to dispatch angels on behalf of my Priest, Prophet, and King (PPK). God, I thank You for positioning me as a Helpmeet suitable to pray for my King's wisdom.

Prayer for My King

Father, Your Word declares, *"For the Lord gives wisdom; From His mouth come knowledge and understanding"*

(Proverbs 2:6, NKJV). Thank You, Lord, for imparting into me wisdom to appropriately pray for my King concerning wisdom in his life. When You created me, Father, You gave me a particular set of skills to cover my King. Lord, You give wisdom; therefore, today, I am asking specifically for wisdom for my King. I decree and declare that my King has the keys to wisdom. God, I understand and know my King is worth it, no matter what I might see in the natural. I pray this is a time of downloading and instructions for my King. Father, I am specifically asking that You open the ears of my King so that he can hear the wisdom being released from Your mouth. I decree and declare that my King understands wisdom is the principal thing *(Proverbs 4:7)*. Not only will my husband receive wisdom, but he will also acquire understanding and knowledge.

Father, unlock the keys to perfect wisdom and give my King the key to understanding wisdom that will unlock things that need to be unlocked. In Jesus' name. I declare because my King walks in perfect wisdom, he will walk in his gift unashamed. I pull down every stronghold that will try to exalt itself above the knowledge of God *(2 Corinthians 10:3-5)*. My King has godly wisdom from above *(James 3:17)*. Father, I pray my King has the knowledge to understand his call and destiny from You.

My King is wise; his decisions are wise; his actions are wise; his behavior is wise; his family is wise; he makes financially wise decisions, in Jesus' name. I slice everything with the sword of the Spirit that tries to come against my King's wisdom. I cut off soul ties and any wrong relationships outside of God's will that are causing my King not to receive the wisdom he needs. I understand wisdom is the principal thing *(Proverbs 4:7)*. Father, download fresh wisdom unto my King, even to the smallest details provide wisdom. Lord, because my King is faithful in the little, make him ruler over much *(Matthew 25:23)*. I decree what I am praying today will be established, in the name of Jesus.

I cut anything that hinders my King from hearing the voice of God and receiving what the Lord has for him. I pray that my husband will have the wisdom to understand spiritual and natural things. I declare he will make wise and accurate choices. My King will have the wisdom to see the enemy, even from afar off. He will have the wisdom and discernment to see the people he should not be around. God, I speak to all the Kings on the earth that their eyes would be open. Open the eyes of their understanding. My King is enlightened today. Wisdom is his portion.

My King has the wisdom to breakthrough and break generational curses. I decree and declare that my King has supernatural wisdom. Lord, if anything hinders my King's eyes and ears from being opened, it is being destroyed by fire. The mind of my King is being renewed. I pray that he will consistently knock and ask for wisdom from You, Lord. Father, You said in Your Word to ask, seek, and knock *(Matthew 7:7),* so today, I ask for wisdom for my King. I speak to the mind of my King and say be transformed right now. I decree the perfect will of God over the life of my King. I decree and declare that he will have the wisdom to love unconditionally. He will have the wisdom to forgive completely and walk circumspectly before the Lord.

I pray that my King is fully equipped to walk in his destiny and purpose with wisdom. He has the wisdom to protect his family and the finances to provide for them. Divine wisdom is downloaded for entrepreneurship, land purchases, contracts, critical decisions, and divine connections. The wisdom downloaded will be straight from heaven and unfiltered. I pray that my King has peace with the wisdom given by the Lord. My King has wisdom like Solomon. He will have wisdom beyond his understanding and his age. My King will impart wisdom into his generation and generations to come. My King will have the wisdom to discern the voice of God, and a stranger he will not follow.

I pray that my King will have the wisdom to know when to rest and when he is physically, mentally, and emotionally tired. My King will understand the sound of God's wisdom. Let wisdom be a distinct sound to my husband's ears. I decree and declare the sound of Holy Spirit and divine wisdom over my King. My King has the wisdom to write his vision down. Lord, take away all distractions from my King that hinder him from receiving wisdom. Father, give my husband the wisdom to share information with the right people. My King's wisdom will not be stolen from him. God, bless him with the strength to protect the information he receives from You. He is only to share with those who You release him to. My King will not be fearful of sharing information with his Helpmeet. We will come together as one and pray over the wisdom God has given us.

I send forth angels to cover my King, in the name of Jesus. I pull down learning disabilities, mental illness, and any residue from past trauma. My King has great wisdom. I decree and declare that every piece of residue that might be present from making poor decisions is being dismantled, in the name of Jesus. I replace hindrances with wisdom, supernatural knowledge, and a supernatural hedge of protection. I curse the spirit of perversion that tries to taint the thinking and decision-making of my King. I decree and declare an impartation of wisdom to cover my King.

My King will receive pure wisdom from God with a clean heart. My King has the wisdom to unlock solutions for the nation. He is a businessman of wisdom. He is a wise leader and understands the legal system. Thank You, Lord, for wisdom. My King will have wisdom concerning the things of marriage. Thank You, Lord, that my King is slow to speak when he is angry. He will have the wisdom to be quiet. My King will have the wisdom to know when something is right or wrong. He has the wisdom to overcome demonic assignments, generational curses, and his past. My King has supernatural wisdom to cover every area of his life. Everything he touches is renewed. Everything he touches is new. He is walking in divine, godly wisdom.

I cover this prayer under the blood of Jesus; no weapon formed against my King and his wisdom shall prosper. He is walking in wisdom like never before from this day forward. He carries a mantle of wisdom on his life for such a time as this. In Jesus' name. Amen.

As a Helpmeet suitable, how can you help your husband receive wisdom from the Lord?

My King's Vision

My King's name is_____.

Key Scripture: *"The oracle of one who hears the words of God, Who sees the vision of the Almighty, Falling down, but having his eyes open and uncovered" (Numbers 24:4, AMP).*

Declaration: I decree and declare that my King has 2020 vision in the spirit and in the natural.

Helpmeet Prayer

God, I am reporting for duty. I am prepared to hear Your instructions, come into agreement with Your will, pray, and ask for forgiveness. Lord God, I am asking for blessings and favor. I am Your vessel that is creating a hedge of protection around my King, family, and me, in the name of Jesus. Father, forgive me of my sins as far as the east is from the west.

I am thankful, Lord God, for that forgiveness. Create in me a clean heart and renew a right spirit within me (*Psalm*

51:10). Your Word declares the effectual fervent prayer of the righteous avails much *(James 5:16)*. Lord, whatever is on Your mind and whatever Holy Spirit tells me I will obey. Lord God, I praise You for doing a new thing in my marriage. Transform me, Lord, in the same areas I pray for my King. Let us both be in one accord to fulfill Your purpose on the earth.

Right now, because we are one, I put the whole armor of God on my King and myself. I put on our helmet of salvation, our breastplate of righteousness, and our loins are girded about with truth. Our feet are shod with the preparation of the gospel of peace *(Ephesians 6:11)*. Our shield of faith is in one hand, and our sword of the Spirit, which is the Word of God, is in the other hand. We have our armor on, and I am ready for battle. No arrow the enemy tries to throw at me will prevail. I am covered under the blood of Jesus. The weapons may form, but they will not prosper *(Isaiah 54:17)*. No scheme, plot, or plan the enemy tries to use to stop me will get past my prayers because I am prepared, and God has my back. In the name of Jesus, I dispatch angels to cover and protect me as I cover my King. God, I thank You that I have the authority to dispatch angels on behalf of my Priest, Prophet, and King (PPK). I pray that my spiritual vision is clear as a Helpmeet as I cover my King. I have my helpmeet army glasses on in the spirit. God, I thank You, for positioning me as a Helpmeet suitable to pray for my King's vision.

Prayer for My King

Lord, I lift up my King_____, in the name of Jesus. God, I pray over his vision. Correct vision is important when walking with You, Lord. I pray for my King's spiritual and natural vision. I bind every assignment of the enemy that may cause him not to see correctly. I decree and declare that my King will have a keen vision. I pray his eyes will be open so he can see the demonic assignments designed to stop him, our family, his gifts, and his calling. As the Helpmeet of my King, I speak the opening of my King's eyes, in the name of Jesus. I declare because my King's eyes are open the enemy's demonic attacks will not hit him. My King will see the attack from afar and be ready in advance. Lord, when my King has vision from You, he can see what the enemy is doing. My King can see what the enemy is plotting and planning against his family, marriage, ministry, and nation.

I decree and declare that the Word of God protects the vision of my King. I pray that His vision will desire to look at God's Word. I decree that the Word of God will cut up every assignment that is hindering the vision of my King. Thank You, Lord, that the scales over the eyes of my King are being removed, in the name of Jesus. As a prophetic act, I rip the scales off my King's eyes. Father, prepare and equip Your son to have 2020 vision in the natural and spiritual. There is no double vision. I bind movement from left to right, in the name of Jesus. My King will press toward the mark of the high calling. His eyes will not only be open naturally and spiritually, but he will also see the vision of God for his life. My King will see exactly the call You have ordained him to walk in, and the path for those he leads, in the name of Jesus.

I speak excellent, clear vision, so my King can follow You, Lord. Consequently, I can follow him as he follows You. God, thank You for making crooked paths straight. Father, You are making my King's path clear because his vision is pointed toward You. Lord, I decree that my King is strong in You and the power of Your might. My King will be able to see and recognize strange women, strange men, and strange assignments, in Jesus' name. I decree there will be no cataracts or blindness in my King's spiritual eyes. He will see clearly.

Father, thank You for performing spiritual eye surgery on my King. You are the great ophthalmologist. I bind every distraction in my King's vision, in the name of Jesus. My King will not be taken off his target; he will not miss the bullseye. God, align the vision of my King with Your kingdom. I declare divine alignment over my King. Lord, I pull down every stronghold that hinders him. God, give him the divine resources in the spirit to clear up any vision problem he may have. Father, whether it is spiritual eye drops, spiritual glasses, or spiritual contact lenses, provide them. My King will see clearly. He will see the glory of God present in his life.

I bind the spirit of adultery. I decree and declare that my King will only have eyes and vision for me as his helpmeet. He is faithful, in the name of Jesus. My King's path is clear and righteous. Father, thank You that my King has vision goals that are created, rooted, and grounded in You. The Word of God shall fulfill these vision goals.

Darkness will no longer be a part of my King's vision. He will see clearly. I decree that my King knows where he is going. He is not lost; he is where he needs to be in God. He is going in the right direction with proficient vision, in the name of Jesus. My King will not get weary of doing well. He will see in the spirit his due harvest at the right time. My

King's vision is clear and secure in You, Lord. He will not fail. The angel of the breakthrough is making the path straight for my King, in Jesus' name. My King is walking on a narrow path because he can see clearly where to go. Father, Your Word declares in *Psalm 119:105*, *"Thy word is a lamp unto my feet and a light unto my path, (KJV)."* Lord, direct my King's path with Your Word as he walks out the vision downloaded into his heart. I decree and declare that my King can see. His vision is clear to walk in his destiny. In the matchless name of Jesus. Amen.

As a Helpmeet suitable, how can you help your husband remain focused in the natural and spiritual? How can you help him see the things of God clearly?

My King's Destiny

My King's name is _____.

Key Scripture: *"In Him also we have received an inheritance [a destiny—we were claimed by God as His own], having been predestined (chosen, appointed beforehand) according to the purpose of Him who works everything in agreement with the counsel and design of His will" (Ephesians 1:11, AMP).*

Declaration: I decree and declare that my King will fulfill the destiny that was predestined for him from the foundation of the world.

Helpmeet Prayer

God, I am reporting for duty. I am prepared to hear Your instructions, to come into agreement with Your will, pray, and ask for forgiveness. Lord God, I am asking for blessings and favor. I am Your vessel that is creating a hedge of protection around my King, family, and me, in the name of Jesus. Father, forgive me of my sins as far as the east is from the west.

I am thankful, Lord God, for that forgiveness. Create in me a clean heart, and renew a right spirit within me (*Psalm 51:10*). Your Word declares the effectual, fervent prayer of the righteous avails much *(James 5:16)*. Lord, whatever is on Your mind, whatever Holy Spirit tells me I will obey. Lord God, I praise You for doing a new thing in my marriage. Transform me, Lord, in the same areas I pray for my King. Let us both be in one accord to fulfill Your purpose on the earth.

Right now, because we are one, I put the whole armor of God on my King and myself. I put on our helmet of salvation, our breastplate of righteousness, and our loins are girded with truth. Our feet are shod with the preparation of the gospel of peace (*Ephesians 6:11*). Our shield of faith is in one hand, and our sword of the Spirit, which is the Word of God, is in the other hand. We have our armor on, and I am prepared for battle. No arrow the enemy tries to throw at me will prevail. I am covered under the blood of Jesus. The weapons may form, but they will not prosper *(Isaiah 54:17)*. No scheme, plot, or plan the enemy tries to use to stop me will get past my prayers because I am prepared, and God has my back. In the name of Jesus, I dispatch angels to cover and protect me as I cover my King. God, I thank You that I have the authority to dispatch angels on behalf of my Priest, Prophet, and King (PPK). God, I thank You for positioning me as a Helpmeet suitable to pray for my King's destiny.

Prayer for My King

Father, I thank You for the life of my Priest, Prophet, and King. Thank You for giving him the strength to walk daily in his destiny and purpose. I decree and declare that my King has wisdom, knowledge, and understanding. Thank You, Lord, that his ears are unplugged so he can hear Your voice. I decree and declare that my King will not follow the voice of a stranger, in the name of Jesus. I bind every assignment that will cause my King not to walk in his destiny. I decree that he will press toward the mark of the high calling in Christ *(Philippians 3:14)*. Nothing sent to his bloodline will be able to hinder him. My King is doing exactly what he was called and destined to do on the earth. In the name of Jesus, every obstacle and distraction is losing its grip on my King's life. He is focused on the will of God for his life. I pull down every stronghold created by sins committed in the past. The Word says in *2 Corinthians 10:4* that the weapons of our warfare are not carnal, but mighty through God to the pulling down of strongholds. My King is delivered to walk in his destiny. I declare he can do all things through Christ who strengthens him (*Philippians 4:13*).

My King is strong in the Lord and the power of His might *(Ephesians 6:10)*.

Lord, I thank You that my King's destiny is covered in the blood of Jesus Christ. He will speak the Word of God. He will speak exactly how God has intended for him to speak. I shut down every assignment on the earth that has been sent to muzzle my King's mouth from speaking the Word of the Lord. The prayers of my King devastate the enemy. My King will pray over and speak into his destiny. Whatever my King speaks according to the will of God shall be established. I bind the spirits of fear, abandonment, and rejection that try to stop my King from moving forward in God. He is being elevated and promoted now in the name of Jesus!

I decree that no sickness will stop my King from walking in his purpose. He is mature and will walk in maturity. My Priest, Prophet, and King will have a mature mindset.

He will make sound decisions all the days of his life. I thank You, Lord, that my King's heart is fixed toward You. Lord, replace the heart of stone with the heart of flesh. I pray that my King will see himself the way God sees him, in the name of Jesus.

I decree and declare a redemption of time. I speak righteousness into the heart and mind of my King. I declare peace over my King's mind. The peace that surpasses all understanding *(Philippians 4:7)*. I speak into my King's life and declare, "Rise up and walk into your purpose!"

I close every breach, in the name of Jesus; Holy Spirit, fill every void. I declare that my King will remove idols from his life and replace them with the glory of God. Father, I pray that my King will hide Your Word in his heart that he may not sin against You *(Psalm 119:11)*.

I declare that my King will walk into his destiny and stand boldly like the King he is. His words are clear and biblical. My King is favored and wears a supernatural crown.

I declare my King is a new creature in Christ. He will fulfill his destiny that he was created for from the foundation of the world. *"Therefore, if any man be in Christ, he is a new creature: old things are passed away; behold, all things are become new" (2 Corinthians 5:17, KJV)*. My King will experience and walk in his newness in God. He is protected by God, covered in the blood, and surrounded by angels to help him fulfill his purpose. In Jesus' name. Amen.

As a Helpmeet suitable, how can you help your husband walk in his purpose and fulfill his destiny?

My King's Spiritual Growth

My King's name is_____.

Key Scripture: *"Therefore let us get past the elementary stage in the teachings about the Christ, advancing on to maturity and perfection and spiritual completeness, [doing this] without laying again a foundation of repentance from dead works and of faith toward God" (Hebrews 6:1, AMP).*

Declaration: I decree and declare that my King is spiritually mature in the principles of the doctrine of Christ.

Helpmeet Prayer

God, I am reporting for duty. I am prepared to hear Your instructions, to come into agreement with Your will, to pray, and to ask for forgiveness. Lord God, I am asking for blessings and favor. I am Your vessel that is creating a hedge of protection around my King, family, and me, in the name of Jesus. Father, forgive me of my sins as far as the east is from the west.

I am thankful, Lord God, for that forgiveness. Create in me a clean heart and renew a right spirit within me (*Psalm 51:10*). Your Word declares the effectual, fervent prayer of the righteous avails much *(James 5:16)*. Lord, whatever is on Your mind, whatever Holy Spirit tells me I will obey. Lord God, I praise You for doing a new thing in my marriage. Transform me, Lord, in the same areas I pray for my King. Let us both be in one accord to fulfill Your purpose on the earth.

Right now, because we are one, I put the whole armor of God on my King and myself. I put on our helmet of salvation, our breastplate of righteousness, and our loins are girded with truth. Our feet are shod with the preparation of the gospel of peace (*Ephesians 6:11*). Our shield of faith is in one hand, and our sword of the Spirit, which is the Word of God, is in the other hand. We have our armor on, and I am prepared for battle. No arrow that the enemy tries to throw at me will prevail. I am covered under the blood of Jesus. The weapons may form, but they will not prosper *(Isaiah 54:17)*. No scheme, plot, or plan the enemy tries to use to stop me will get past my prayers because I am prepared, and God has my back. In the name of Jesus, I dispatch angels to cover and protect me as I cover my King. God, I thank You that I have the authority to dispatch angels on behalf of my Priest, Prophet, and King (PPK). God, I thank You for positioning me as a Helpmeet suitable to pray for my King's spiritual growth.

Prayer for My King

Father, I thank You that You are the most excellent teacher of all things. I pray, Lord, that You will impart spiritual principles into my King. Increase his knowledge in the things of God and the kingdom to make him spiritually mature in You. I decree and declare as my King spends time with You, Lord, that he is growing and disciplined in the spirit. I declare that my King is walking in authority and power because he is wise in the things of God. I declare that my King has all the power over the enemy. *"Behold, I give you the authority to trample on serpents and scorpions, and over all the power of the enemy and nothing shall by any means hurt you" (Luke 10:19, NKJV)*. Thank You, Lord, that my King sits in heavenly places with You *(Ephesians 2:6)*. He has all knowledge of his authority on the earth and spiritual realm. I decree that my King knows who he is in Christ. He walks in humility and oneness with the Lord. Spiritual maturity is my King's portion. I decree and declare that he hungers and thirsts for righteousness *(Matthew 6:5)*. My husband's prayers are of a fervent man of God *(James 5:16)*. Lord, because my King is spiritually mature, things of the flesh do not entice him. He is rightly positioned with God. My King is not a man of the past, but one who hopes in his future.

My King is leading others to grow spiritually in You, Lord. I bind the spirit of arrested development. I bind spiritual immaturity, in the name of Jesus. My King is mature in the spirit, as well as his declarations and decrees. He is mature in his praise and worship. The strength of the Lord is upon my King to do good and serve the Lord with maturity.

My King is aware of the enemy's tricks and resists the enemy. My King is protected by God, in the name of Jesus. Lord, because my King is growing in the spirit, grace him to walk in his spiritual gifts, his anointing, and his spiritual growth. Lord, I thank You that You are my husband's shield, and the blood of Jesus covers him.

My King is a man of his word. He studies and meditates on the Word of God day and night. The Word of God shall never depart from his mouth but be an aid to his spiritual growth *(Joshua 1:8)*. My King is a man of worship, and he reverences the Lord. My husband is not afraid to lay prostrate before the Lord and give Him glory. I pray that my King will study to show himself approved. *"Study to shew thyself approved unto God, a workman that needeth not to be ashamed, rightly dividing the word of truth" (2 Timothy 2:15, KJV)*. My King will have a heart for spiritual maturity, in the name of Jesus. I speak supernatural growth that will cause favor to shield my King and open the door for promotion. I speak spiritual doctorate degrees over my King.

Father, accelerate my King in the spiritual for Your benefit and glory.

I cut soul ties that try to hinder the growth of my King. He will have spiritual maturity in his eyes and ears. He will be accountable for what he lets into his spirit. My husband is mature enough to handle his business and cover his family in prayer. He will not be intimidated by help but will embrace the help God sends. Thank You, Lord, that my King understands covenant and what it means to be in covenant with You and his Helpmeet. My King is disciplined in the Lord and spiritually mature. In Jesus' name, Amen.

As a Helpmeet suitable how can you continue to help your husband grow spiritually in the Lord?

MY KING'S HEART

My King's name is_____.

Key Scripture: *"Moreover, I will give you a new heart and put a new spirit within you, and I will remove the heart of stone from your flesh and give you a heart of flesh" (Ezekiel 36:26, AMP).*

Declaration: I decree and declare that my King has a new heart. He has hidden the Word in his heart to live according to the will of God.

Helpmeet Prayer

God, I am reporting for duty. I am prepared to hear Your instructions, to come into agreement with Your will, pray, and ask for forgiveness. Lord God, I am asking for blessings and favor. I am Your vessel that is creating a hedge of protection around my King, family, and me, in the name of Jesus. Father, forgive me of my sins as far as the east is from the west.

I am thankful, Lord God, for that forgiveness. Create in me a clean heart and renew a right spirit within me (*Psalm 51:10*). Your Word declares the effectual, fervent prayer of the righteous avails much *(James 5:16)*. Lord, whatever is on Your mind, whatever Holy Spirit tells me I will obey. Lord God, I praise You for doing a new thing in my marriage. Transform me, Lord, in the same areas I pray for my King. Let us both be in one accord to fulfill Your purpose on the earth.

Right now, because we are one, I put the whole armor of God on my King and myself. I put on our helmet of salvation, our breastplate of righteousness, and our loins are girded about with truth. Our feet are shod with the preparation of the gospel of peace (*Ephesians 6:11*). Our shield of faith is in one hand, and our sword of the Spirit, which is the Word of God, is in the other hand. We have our armor on, and I am prepared and ready for battle. No arrow the enemy tries to throw at me will prevail. I am covered under the blood of Jesus. The weapons may form, but they will not prosper *(Isaiah 54:17)*. No scheme, plot, or plan the enemy tries to use to stop me will get past my prayers because I am prepared, and God has my back. In the name of Jesus, I dispatch angels to cover and protect me as I cover my King. God, I thank You that I have the authority to dispatch angels on behalf of my Priest, Prophet, and King (PPK). I thank You for positioning me as a Helpmeet suitable to pray for my King's heart.

Prayer for My King

Oh, King of my heart. I am coming to You on behalf of my King. Thank You for what You have already done. Create in my King a clean heart and renew in him a right spirit *(Psalm 51:10)*. I pray that my King's heart will line up with the Word of God. I pray that he will love unconditionally, and his heart will turn toward You. I decree and declare that my King's heart is pure and holy. His heart is softened, in the name of Jesus. Lord, protect my King's heart. I come against past trauma that will try to hinder the heart of my King. I decree as I pray for my King's heart, this will be a heart check for him. Father, allow my husband to reflect on the things in his heart that may need to change so he can live according to Your will and purpose.

God, You are the great cardiologist in the spirit; do surgery on the heart of my King, in the name of Jesus. And because You are the great cardiologist. You hold my King's heart in Your hand. Lord, break down and chisel the hardness of my King's heart. Your Word declares in *Ezekiel 36:26 (NKJV)*, *"I will give you a new heart and put a new spirit within you; I will take the heart of stone out of your flesh and give you a heart of flesh."* Thank You, Lord, that my husband has a heart of flesh; therefore, he has the heart to forgive. Thank You, Lord, for supernatural heart surgery. Thank You, Lord, for the heart transplant of my King.

I decree and declare that my King will have the heart to receive the love of God. My King will speak of how great God is. My King will speak love, peace, and joy over his family, marriage, and future. My King speaks over his purpose and destiny with love. For out of the abundance of the heart his mouth speaks *(Luke 6:45)*.

I plead the blood of Jesus over every part of my King's heart. Every word out of my husband's heart is spoken in love. I pray that he loves his helpmeet. I decree that the desires of my husband's heart match the desires of Your heart, God. Thank You, King of kings, for Your grace over my King's life.

The past of my King's heart is being washed away, and all things are being made new, in the name of Jesus. My King's heart will continue to be softened. God, I pray that my husband will not lean unto his own understanding, but he will acknowledge You in all his ways. Lord, direct the path of my King for Your glory *(Proverbs 3:5-6).*

I cut and sever everything that is trying to come against the heart of my King, in Jesus' name. I use the sword of the Spirit to cut every soul tie that is trying to connect him to the wrong spirit. I cut the soul tie that is connecting him to any strange man or woman. I cut the soul tie that is connecting my King to generational curses. I reverse every curse spoken over my King's heart. I speak a heart shift now over my King, in the name of Jesus.

Father, I declare my King will no longer feel separated from the love of God or the love of his helpmeet. No longer will he feel disconnected from the love of his parents. I speak a heart of forgiveness over my King. Father, give my husband a heart to pray for those who despitefully use him. Give him the heart to look back and say, "I forgive them," in the name of Jesus. Father, God, forgive me for not speaking to the heart of my King appropriately. May my words to him be spoken in love.

My King has the heart and strength to break off unforgiveness and rejection. My King will understand how to love unconditionally like You, Lord. Satan, you cannot have my King's heart! In Jesus' name. My King will hear the voice of the Lord and a stranger's voice he will not follow *(John 10:5)*.

I declare that my King will hide the Word in his heart that he may not sin against You, Lord *(Psalm 119:11)*. The heart of my King is fixed toward You, Lord. Father, because my King's heart is right toward You, he will walk in his five-fold ministry gift. He is a man of valor. The heart of my King is open to receive from the Lord. I speak righteousness into his heart. The heart of my King is humble. Lord, pour Your love into his heart; this is what he needs in this season. My husband is overflowing with love in this season.

I declare the supernatural love of God will allow my King to operate in his new heart. Lord, teach me how to take care of my husband's new heart; I will protect, cover, love, honor, and respect the heart of my King. I will create the right environment in our home for the new heart to settle. Our home will be conducive to deliverance for continued health and healing. In the mighty name of Jesus. Amen.

As a Helpmeet suitable, how can you continue to help your husband operate in his new heart?

My King's Strength

My King's name is_____.

Key Scripture: *"The LORD is my strength and my [impenetrable] shield; My heart trusts [with unwavering confidence] in Him, and I am helped; Therefore my heart greatly rejoices, And with my song I shall thank Him and praise Him" (Psalm 28:7, AMP).*

Declaration: I decree and declare that my King is clothed in the strength of the Lord. He is shielded by God all the days of his life. I decree that my King will always look for strength in the Lord, and he will be helped.

Helpmeet Prayer

God, I am reporting for duty. I am prepared to hear Your instructions, to come into agreement with Your will, pray, and ask for forgiveness. Lord God, I am asking for blessings and favor. I am Your vessel that is creating a hedge of protection around my King, family, and me, in the name of Jesus. Father, forgive me of my sins as far as the east is from the west.

I am thankful, Lord God, for that forgiveness. Create in me a clean heart and renew a right spirit within me (*Psalm 51:10*). Your Word declares the effectual, fervent prayer of the righteous avails much *(James 5:16)*. Lord, whatever is on Your mind, whatever Holy Spirit tells me I will obey. Lord God, I praise You for doing a new thing in my marriage. Transform me, Lord, in the same areas I pray for my King. Let us both be in one accord to fulfill Your purpose on the earth.

Right now, because we are one, I put the whole armor of God on my King and myself. I put on our helmet of salvation, our breastplate of righteousness, and our loins are girded with truth. Our feet are shod with the preparation of the gospel of peace (*Ephesians 6:11*). Our shield of faith is in one hand, and our sword of the Spirit, which is the Word of God, is in the other hand. We have our armor on, and I am ready for battle. No arrow the enemy tries to throw at me will prevail. I am covered under the blood of Jesus. The weapons may form, but they will not prosper *(Isaiah 54:17)*. No scheme, plot, or plan the enemy tries to use to stop me will get past my prayers because I am prepared, and God has my back. In the name of Jesus, I dispatch angels, to cover and protect me as I cover my King. God, I thank You that I have the authority to dispatch angels on behalf of my Priest, Prophet, and King (PPK). I thank You for positioning me as a Helpmeet suitable to pray for my King's strength.

Prayer for My King

Oh, God, my strength and my shield. I come to You on behalf of my King. I speak strength over him, in the name of

Jesus. I speak strength to who he is, strength to his identity, strength to be a good father, strength to be a good husband, and strength to grow, in the name of Jesus.

I come against the spirit of arrested development that tries to prevent my King from being strong enough to do what he is called to do. Arrested development will no longer have an entryway into my King's life, in the name of Jesus. My King has the strength to understand and operate in spiritual and natural responsibility. He is a kingdom man and walks in his authority. I bind every assignment of stress and anxiety that causes my King to stay immature in spirit.

I decree and declare strength over my King's mind, decision-making, and strength to control his attitude, in Jesus' name. I speak spiritual strength over my King to push his way through concerning the things of God. My King will have the strength to make the right decisions concerning the church, prayer, and studying God's Word to show himself approved.

I speak strength to his mindset and ability to do Your will, Lord. My King is powerful in his thought process. I speak strength over him so he has the ability to increase and improve in his role as a husband and father. My King will improve in his communication; everything about my King is being strengthened now. I speak supernatural strength over him. I expect to see him strong in every area of his life. My King will be strong physically and mentally, in Jesus' name. God, because You are strong, so is my husband. I crush the assignment of the enemy that will cause my King to be weak. My Priest, Prophet, and King is strong and powerful, in the name of Jesus. I decree that my King is strong on his job and study. He has the spiritual tenacity to keep going. I declare that he is successful because he is strong.

Jehovah Rapha, the God that heals in Jesus' name, I speak healing strength over my King. I decree and declare he will not give up. He is strong enough to handle every attack thrown his way. The attacks of perversion, addiction, and generational curses are being broken now! In Jesus' name.

I declare that my King is strong enough to be successful and committed to the things of God. My husband is committed to serving God, as well as being a kingdom husband and a kingdom man. My King is strong enough to stay committed to one relationship with his helpmeet and being a committed father to his children.

I decree that my King is strong enough to take care of himself, as well as to do and fulfill the will of God. My King is strong enough to overcome his past. He will use the tools of God to stay strong in the Lord. My King will use his tools of speaking in tongues, praise, and the whole armor of God to remain strong. *"For the weapons of our warfare are not carnal but mighty in God for pulling down strongholds" (2 Corinthians 10:4, NKJV).*

I speak spiritual strength over my King, in the name of Jesus. I declare that my King walks in strength. He walks in authority and humility. Thank You, Lord, that my King is no longer walking in disobedience; he is strong enough to understand and follow instructions.

My King is strong enough to maintain his deliverance and

walk in wholeness with God. My King will walk in victory. King, arise! In the name of Jesus. Lord, Your Word declares, *"Finally, my brethren, be strong in the Lord and in the power of His might" (Ephesians 6:10, NKJV)*. I declare that my King is strong in the Lord!

I decree and declare that my King is strong enough to walk in the assignment of the Lord for his life. I declare that my King can do all things through Christ who gives him strength *(Philippians 4:13)*. I thank You, Lord, that I serve the God of the impossible and my husband can do impossible things through You (*Matthew 19:26*).

I annihilate every assignment of the enemy that tries to take the strength of my King. I put on the strength of God today and declare that my King is strong! In the name of Jesus. Amen.

As a Helpmeet suitable, how can you continue to help your husband walk in the strength of the Lord?

About the Author

Yvette Benton is an apostolic voice with a Deborah anointing. She is anointed to not only pray but also train other Helpmeets to pray and believe God's Word for their marriages, families, and destinies. She and her husband Gerald have a testimony of marriage restoration through unconditional love and the power of spiritual warfare prayers. They have been married for over 21 years and now have a unique team ministry. Their marriage ministry Gerald & Yvette Ministries (GYM) teaches the body of Christ how to fulfill the roles of a Priest, Prophet, King (PPK), and a Helpmeet suitable. This is the foundation of a kingdom family.

Contact Yvette Benton

Facebook: Gerald and Yvette Ministries
YouTube: Gerald and Yvette Ministries
Instagram: @Gym_Ministries
Twitter: @GeraldandYvette
Website: www.GeraldandYvette.com
Email: Geraldandyvette@gmail.com

www.ingramcontent.com/pod-product-compliance
Lightning Source LLC
LaVergne TN
LVHW051507070426
835507LV00022B/2965